ROTARY CUTTING
with
Alex Anderson

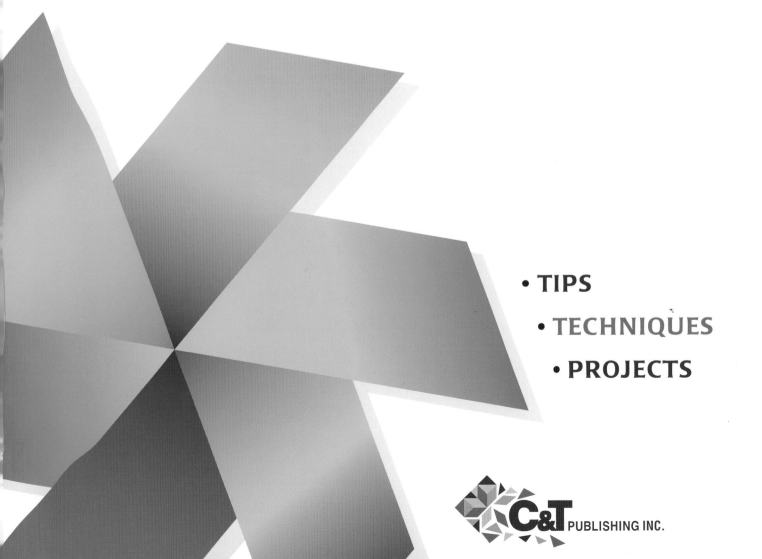

- **TIPS**
- **TECHNIQUES**
- **PROJECTS**

C&T PUBLISHING INC.

©1999 Alex Anderson
Illustrations and How-to Photography ©1999
C&T Publishing, Inc.

DEVELOPMENTAL EDITOR: Liz Aneloski
TECHNICAL EDITORS: Joyce Engels Lytle
and Sally Lanzarotti
COPY EDITOR: Vera Tobin
DESIGN DIRECTION: Kathy Lee
DESIGNER: Micaela Miranda Carr
ILLUSTRATORS: Alan McCorkle and
Jay Richards
PHOTOGRAPHY: Sharon Risedorph
Cover Photo taken at the Sladky's home
(Alex's parents) by John Bagley

Published by C&T Publishing, Inc., P.O. Box
1456, Lafayette, California 94549

ATTENTION TEACHERS:
C&T Publishing, Inc. encourages you to use
this book as a text for teaching. Contact us at
800-284-1114 or www.ctpub.com for more
information about the C&T Teachers Program.

Trademarked (™) and Registered Trademarked
(®) names are used throughout this book.
Rather than use the symbols with every occur-
rance of a trademark and registered trademark
name, we are using the names only in an edi-
torial fashion and to the benefit of the owner,
with no intention of infringement.

We take great care to ensure that the information included in this book is accurate and presented in good faith, but no warranty is
provided nor results guaranteed. Since we
have no control over the choice of materials or
procedures used, neither the author nor C&T
Publishing, Inc. shall have any liability to any
person or entity with respect to any loss or
damage caused directly or indirectly by the
information contained in this book.

Library of Congress Cataloging-in-Publication
Data

Anderson, Alex.
        Rotary cutting with Alex Anderson :
tips, techniques, and projects
    / Alex Anderson.
            p.   cm.
        ISBN 1-57120-066-5 (pbk.)
            1. Patchwork.   2. Patchwork—
Patterns.   3. Rotary cutting.
    I. Title
    TT835.A522   1999
    746.44'5—dc21
                        98-46591
                        CIP

Printed in China

10 9 8 7 6 5 4 3

Acknowledgments

THANKS TO:

RJR Fashion Fabrics, P&B Textiles, and
Robert Kaufmann Company, Inc. for your
wonderful fabrics; Olfa Products and
Omnigrid, Inc. for great tools; Paula Reid for
your friendship and fine workmanship: and
Karan Slates, whose friendship I treasure.
Without all of your support and generosity
this project would not have been possible.

Dedication

To my friends and
co-workers at C&T
Publishing; it's always a joy
to work with you. Your
attention to quality and
team spirit is an
inspiration to me.

Contents

Introduction

Quilters
celebrate the
day rotary cutters,
mats, and rulers were
introduced to the world of
quilting. I can still remember my
first experience using a rotary cutter. It
was the oddest tool I had ever seen! But, like
telephones, wind-up baby swings, and take-out food,
I can't imagine my life without it! With its ease and speed
of multiple-layer cutting, as well as its accuracy, rotary cutting
revolutionized my world of quiltmaking.

If quilting is an interest you are investigating (and of course I
encourage you to do so), or you already consider yourself
quite seasoned, but are not yet familiar with the
benefits and intricacies of rotary cutting, this
book is for you. As you become familiar
with its proper use, I guarantee it
will change your approach to
quiltmaking and you
will love the
rotary cutter
as I do!

Supplies

ROTARY CUTTERS

What exactly is a rotary cutter? A rotary cutter is a rolling razor blade mounted on a plastic handle. It is extremely sharp! There are several different brands and sizes available today. To date my favorite is the Olfa rotary cutter. I like how it handles and can be used both left- and right-handed without re-positioning the blade. Olfa cutters come in three sizes: small, medium, and large. The small cutter is appropriate for small scale or miniature quiltmaking and for patterns with curves. With the small cutter you can cut up to two layers of 100% cotton with insured accuracy. The medium cutter will allow you to cut up to four layers of 100% cotton at once. For the dedicated quilter, who finds her- or himself enjoying many hours of piecing, the large cutter is a must. It is much faster, and can cut up to six layers at once. For your first purchase, if it is within your budget, treat yourself to the large cutter. Otherwise the medium size is fine. In addition, Olfa manufactures the Olfa Deluxe rotary cutter. It is ergonomically designed for a comfortable grip and has an improved safety latch.

CARE AND STORAGE OF ROTARY CUTTERS

- Make sure the mat is free of pins and odd objects when cutting. If you run over a pin while cutting, the blade will be nicked and ruined.

- Periodically clean the blade.

- Replace the blade when it becomes dull or nicked.

Cleaning or Blade Replacement

To maximize the longevity of your rotary cutter, periodically you will need to clean it to remove lint build-up between the blade and blade cover. You will also find it necessary to replace the old blade when it becomes nicked (it skips spots when cutting) or dull (it seems unable to cut without a lot of pressure). Always use blades that are designed specifically for your brand of cutter.

These cleaning and blade replacement instructions are for the Olfa rotary cutter. If you are using another brand, pay close attention to the assembly order as you take it apart. To disassemble the Olfa cutter first make sure that the blade cover is in the closed position. Unscrew the small back bolt and take each part off one piece at a time. Lay the pieces out in the order they come off the unit.

Safety

- Keep the blade away from inquisitive hands. It is VERY sharp, even when not in use.

- When not cutting, always have the blade cover in the closed position.

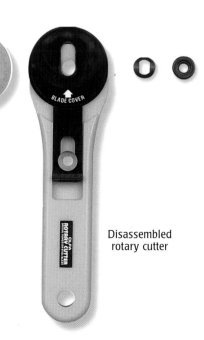

Disassembled rotary cutter

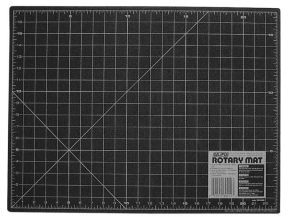

Proper way to
hold the blade

It is very important that you use extreme caution when taking a rotary cutter apart. Remember, you are working with a circular razor blade. Always handle the blade by holding it by the two flat sides of the blade, not the sharp edge!

To clean the rotary cutter once you have disassembled it, wipe the blade, blade cover, and barrel of the plastic holder to clean off lint and residue. Put one drop of sewing machine oil between the blade and the blade cover.

To replace with a new blade, take the old blade and put it into the package that the new blade came out of. Tape the package securely before throwing the old blade away. This will help safeguard the disposal of the old blade. Place the new blade in position.

After replacing or cleaning the blade reassemble the pieces in the correct order. The only tricky part is that the concave curve on the little cupped washer should face away from the handle.

There are mail order companies that will sharpen your rotary cutting blades for you. Inexpensive blade sharpeners are available to use at home for a quick fix to sharpen the blades yourself.

ROTARY CUTTING MATS

For safety and longevity, always use your rotary cutter with a rotary cutting mat and rotary cutting ruler. A rotary cutting mat is a self-healing plastic mat designed specifically for rotary cutting. NEVER try to skimp and use another cutting surface (such as linoleum or wood). This is dangerous and your rotary cutting blade will be ruined in no time.

For accurate cutting it is best to purchase a mat with a grid. There are several brands and sizes available. I recommend that you start with an 18" x 24" size Olfa mat or 17" x 23" Omnigrid mat. For the minimal price difference between the medium- and smaller-size mats, I think it is worth it to own the medium-size one. The smaller mat is great for workshops and the largest mat is wonderful if you have a designated work area. Eventually you will own several sizes.

Rotary cutting mat

CARE AND STORAGE OF ROTARY CUTTING MATS

◆ Always keep the mat out of direct sunlight and never leave it in a hot car. It will warp from the heat and become unusable.

◆ Do not store the mat on its side or rolled up for any extended period of time; it will develop a permanent bend.

◆ Wash periodically with warm soapy water or window cleaner.

ROTARY CUTTING RULERS

Thick, translucent acrylic rotary cutting rulers are designed to be used with rotary cutters. Never use a ruler that is not designed specifically to be used with a rotary cutter; not only is it dangerous, but it can ruin your blade.

For your first ruler and for general use, look for a ruler that has ⅛" increments marked both horizontally and vertically. To make most of the quilts in this book, the ruler must also have 45° and 60° markings. I recommend starting with the 6" x 12" size Omnigrid; it is an excellent all-purpose ruler with all the necessary angles.

At first this ruler might seem a little bit overwhelming. Simply think of the 1" increments as eight small parts and count over the desired measurements one eighth at a time. This helps dissolve any math insecurities. Don't be surprised that your collection of rulers will grow as you become familiar with rotary cutting.

CARE AND STORAGE OF ROTARY CUTTING RULERS

- Most rulers have a hole for hanging storage. I hang mine from a nail on the wall. If you can't hang them up, store them out of the way on a flat surface to avoid breakage.

- Wash periodically with warm soapy water or window cleaner. If necessary you can also clean them with rubbing alcohol. Do not use nail polish remover, as it will remove the ruler markings.

Rotary ruler

⅛" increments

FABRIC

As you know, quilts are not usually created overnight. What a shame it would be to have less-than-desirable results because the fabric was of poor quality. Your quilts should be around for generations to come to be enjoyed visually and to be able to stand up to multiple washings when lovingly used. Therefore always use the best 100% cotton fabric available to you. Less expensive cottons are loosely woven with a lesser thread count per inch. They will cause you problems in the end since they may stretch and distort. Stay away from cotton/polyester blends. Not only will they shrink and distort when pressed, but they can be difficult to hand quilt through.

The quilts in this book celebrate my passion for fabric and the quest to use as many different fabrics in one quilt as possible. If you are a new quilter your collection may not allow as many random choices. If you have been quilting for a few years I'm sure your fabric stash will support these projects. Be willing to stretch and experiment with new color and fabric combinations. This will help you become confident with fabric selection. The main thing is to play and have fun with your fabric.

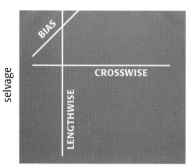

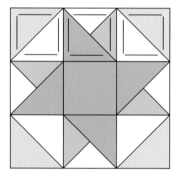

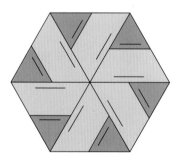

Fabric grain lines

Star block showing
grain direction

Whirligig block showing
grain direction

GRAIN

In quiltmaking, understanding the grain of the fabric is very important. When fabric is produced the threads are woven in two directions. The length of the fabric is called the lengthwise grain and has little if any stretch. The width of the fabric is called the crosswise grain and has a little stretch. Straight of grain refers to either the lengthwise or crosswise grain. When you cut diagonally, across the grain (no matter what the angle), you are cutting on the bias. As you learn to cut the different shapes in this book it is very important to understand where the exposed bias edges are.

Bias edges must be handled, sewn, and pressed with care since they stretch easily. The outside edge of your finished block should be on the straight of grain whenever possible. When it is not possible to have the outside edge on the straight of grain, stitch around the outside of the block ⅛" in from the raw edge to prevent stretching.

Periodically a fabric may be printed "off grain." This means that the print of the fabric is not registered properly on the grain. In this case I let the print of the fabric dictate the cut, understanding that this is a compromise solution.

The two long finished edges of the fabric are called the selvages. Always cut off the selvage edges. If left on, the selvages can cause distortion of the block and they are difficult to hand quilt through.

PREPARING THE FABRIC

There are many different schools of thought as to whether or not you should prewash your fabric. My theory is that you should. Here are my reasons:

◆ When 100% cotton fabric is washed and dried, shrinkage can occur, causing puckers and distortion of the quilt.

◆ Dye from darker color fabrics has been known to "run" (migrate) to the lighter fabrics.

◆ Fabric is treated with chemicals. I do not think it is healthy to breathe or handle these chemicals over an extended period of time.

One of the objections to prewashing is that sometimes the fabric seems to lose its body. For ease of piecing, it's important that the different fabrics you use have the same body. If the fabrics seem to handle differently, use either spray starch or sizing when pressing the fabric in preparation for cutting. Never spray starch a shape that has already been cut, and always make sure the fabric is totally dry before cutting into it.

8

Rotary Cutting

SAFETY

Before you experience this fabulous tool by actually cutting into fabric, I must again caution you that this is an extremely dangerous tool that must be used and stored properly to ensure safety. Here are the rules:

◆ Always store your cutter with the blade cover closed.

◆ Always close the blade cover after every cut. This motion should become second nature.

◆ Keep your cutter out of reach of all inquisitive hands, especially young children and husbands wrapping Christmas gifts.

◆ Wear shoes when cutting. I once had a student visit the emergency room after dropping the cutter on her foot. Ouch!

GETTING STARTED

It is important to learn the correct way to hold your tools for your personal safety. Incorrect hand position can result in cut fingers or carpal tunnel syndrome, so to protect yourself, learn to cut the correct way.

Proper position
left-handed

Hold the rotary cutter in the hand you write with. Place the handle in your palm and wrap your hand around it. Place your index finger on the bumpy part of the handle and` lift your elbow slightly.

MAGIC NUMBERS

On the following pages you will learn how to cut a variety of shapes used in quiltmaking. The shapes presented in this book are listed in order of difficulty.

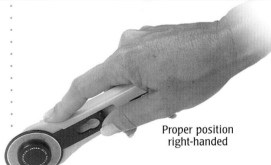

Proper position
right-handed

Each shape has magic (rotary cutting) numbers that are consistently used when determining what size to cut the different shapes. Different shapes have different numbers. This is because of the angles in the shapes. Unless you want to worry about trigonometry, just be assured that they work. As you become familiar with rotary cutting, these numbers will become second nature. Here are the two basic rules for using magic numbers.

1. The numbers will only work with ¼" seam allowances.

2. Measure the finished size of the desired shape and then add the magic number. This measurement will be the size to cut your shape with seam allowances included.

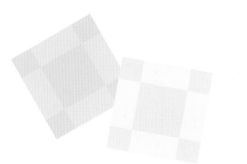

TIPS

◆ Practice cutting scraps of fabric with the rotary cutter, mat, and ruler before you try cutting shapes for your quilt.

◆ When rotary cutting it is a good idea, whenever possible, to position your fabric and ruler so the ruler covers the finished shape being cut. This will help prevent your accidentally cutting into the finished shape if you make a mistake. However, as the shapes become more complicated it is more practical to rotate the ruler (leaving the finished shape unprotected) rather than rotating the cutting mat or fabric for each cut. The choice is yours.

PROBLEM SOLVING

If the fabric isn't cutting nicely:

◆ The blade is dull or nicked and it needs to be replaced.

◆ You need to exert more pressure on the cutter.

◆ You are trying to cut through too many layers of fabric.

◆ The tension is either too loose or too tight on the blade assembly. Adjust by loosening or tightening the bolt.

◆ The blade is not being positioned straight up and down, directly against the ruler.

If you find the bottom edge of the fabric is not being cut, extend the edge of ruler past the bottom edge of the fabric and start your cut on the mat, then proceed onto the fabric.

CONCLUSION

Before you know it, you will be comfortable with the cutting process. The accuracy and speed of rotary cutting is a phenomenon that changed the face of quiltmaking only two decades ago. If I could only take five quilting items to a deserted tropical island, I can assure you that my rotary cutting tools would be near the top of the list. That is, of course, after my fabric collection! Until we meet, Happy Quilting.

Alex Anderson

SQUARING UP THE FABRIC

Yahoo! It's time to get started. First you must make the initial cut to clean off the uneven raw edge. This is called "squaring up" the fabric.

It is important that the fabric be smooth and flat with the folded edges lined up parallel to one another. This will ensure that your cut strips are straight, not "V" shaped. The raw edge of the fabric will most likely be uneven.

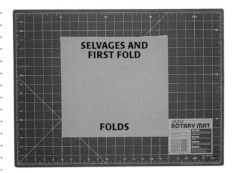

1. Fold the fabric selvage to selvage and then fold again. This will give you four layers to cut through. Position the fabric on the mat, keeping the folded edges of the fabric in line with the horizontal lines on the mat. (Avoid letting any fabric hang off the edge of the table.)

Tips

◆ Always cut at a 90 degree angle, directly away from your body. It is much more comfortable to cut from the hip, rather than directly in the center of your body.

◆ Place the silver side of the rotary cutter blade directly against the edge of the ruler.

Left-handed   Right-handed

2. To clean off the uneven raw edge, line up the vertical and horizontal marks on the ruler on or parallel to the grid on the mat. Place the ruler about ½" over the raw edge of the fabric. All three—the mat, ruler, and fabric—need to be aligned on or parallel to both the mat and ruler grids.

3. Hold down the ruler with your hand in the center in a spread position, using your fingertips only. Make sure none of your fingers are over the edge of the ruler on the side where you will be cutting. Rest your pinkie finger on the outside edge of the ruler (on the side where you won't be cutting) to balance the ruler and keep it from shifting. Expose the blade of the cutter by pulling the black blade cover back. The blade is now exposed and extremely dangerous.

4. Position the rolling razor blade with the silver side directly against the edge of the ruler. The bolt of the rotary cutter is on the outside. The cutting blade should be straight up and down against the ruler, not tilted.

5. Roll the rotary cutter blade next to the ruler on the mat. Make a single pass through the entire piece of the fabric and immediately close the blade cover. This cannot be emphasized enough! Make sure you cut away the uneven raw edges on all four layers of fabric. The fabric is now squared up. This step is necessary before cutting all shapes.

Caution

◆ The blade should ONLY be exposed when it's in use.

CUTTING STRIPS

MAGIC NUMBER

A strip is the most basic unit used in rotary cutting. Many of the other shapes begin with a cut strip.

NOTE: If the strip is wider than the ruler, use the lines on the mat to get the desired width.

CUTTING SQUARES

MAGIC NUMBER

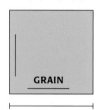

FINISHED SIZE + ½"

Squares are simply strips cut into smaller units.

CUTTING RECTANGLES

MAGIC NUMBERS

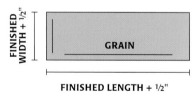

FINISHED LENGTH + ½"

Rectangles are simply strips cut into smaller units.

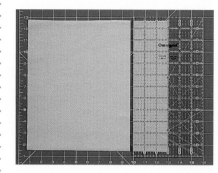
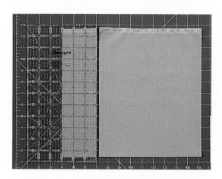

1. Square up the fabric (page 11). Move the ruler over the desired finished strip width plus ½", lining up the vertical measurement on the ruler with the trimmed edge of the fabric. Make sure the fabric and ruler are also in alignment with the grid on the mat.
2. Cut the strip.

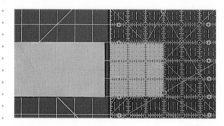
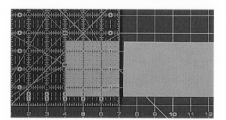

1. Square up the fabric (page 11). Cut the strip the desired finished size + ½".
2. Reposition the strip horizontally, on or parallel to one of the mat's gridlines. Cutting through the folded strip will give you four shapes from each cut. If you require fewer than four shapes, open the strip.
3. Trim off the uneven edges to square up the end.
4. Move the ruler over the desired finished length + ½" (this measurement will be the same as the width you cut the strip) and cut.

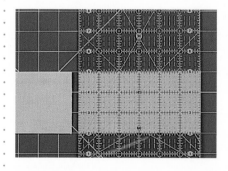
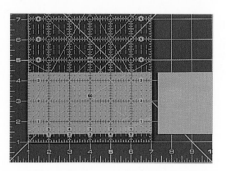

1. Square up the fabric (page 11). Cut the strip the desired finished width + ½".
2. Reposition the strip horizontally, on or parallel to one of the mat's gridlines. Cutting through the folded strip will give you four shapes from each cut. If you require fewer than four shapes, open the strip.
3. Trim off the uneven edges to square up the end.
4. Move the ruler over the desired finished length + ½" and cut.

CUTTING HALF-SQUARE TRIANGLES

MAGIC NUMBER

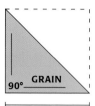

FINISHED SIZE + ⅞"

Triangles can be tricky. Both half-square triangles and quarter-square triangles have 90° angles in one corner. Although they look the same, the difference between the two triangles is where the straight of the grain ends up. It is important to understand the difference between the two triangles because you always want the outside edge of the block on the straight of grain. Which triangle you use can determine the fate of your block. Both of these triangles start with a square.

The half-square triangle has the two sides adjacent to the 90° angle on the straight of grain. The quarter-square triangle has the side opposite the 90° angle on the straight of grain.

 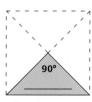

Half-square
triangle   Quarter-square
triangle

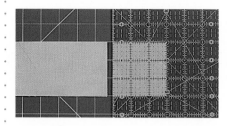 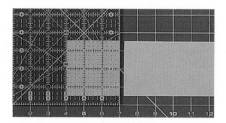

1. Square up the fabric (page 11). Cut the strip the desired finished width + ⅞" (page 12).

2. Reposition the strip horizontally, on or parallel to one of the mat's gridlines.

3. Trim off the uneven edges to square up the end.

4. Move the ruler over the desired finished length + ⅞" and cut a square.

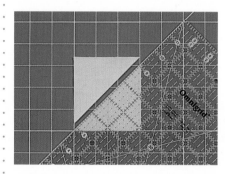 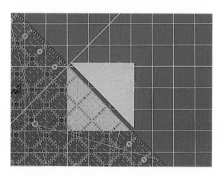

5. Position the ruler corner to corner and cut the square in half diagonally.

CUTTING QUARTER-SQUARE TRIANGLES

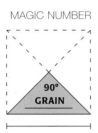

MAGIC NUMBER

90°
GRAIN

FINISHED SIZE + 1¼"

Triangles can be tricky. Both half-square triangles and quarter-square triangles have 90° angles in one corner. Although they look the same, the difference between the two triangles is where the straight of grain ends up. It is important to understand the difference between the two triangles because you always want the outside edge of the block on the straight of grain. Which triangle you use can determine the fate of your block. Both of these triangles start with a square.

The half-square triangle has the two sides adjacent to the 90° angle on the straight of grain. The quarter-square triangle has the side opposite the 90° angle on the straight of grain.

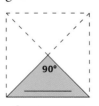

Half-square
triangle

Quarter-square
triangle

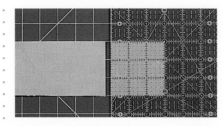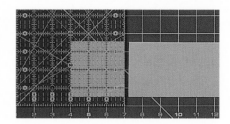

1. Square up the fabric (page 11). Cut the strip the desired finished size + 1¼" (page 12).

2. Reposition the strip horizontally, on or parallel to one of the mat's gridlines.

3. Trim off the uneven edges to square up the end.

4. Move the ruler over the desired finished length + 1¼" and cut a square.

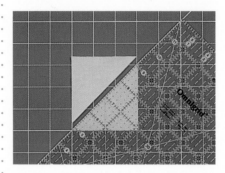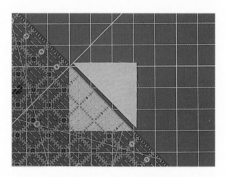

5. Position the ruler corner to corner and cut the square in half diagonally.

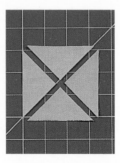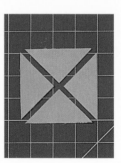

6. Cut the square in half diagonally a second time.

CUTTING 45°
TRAPEZOIDS

MAGIC NUMBERS

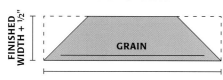

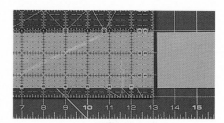

The 45° trapezoids are simply rectangles with each end cut on a 45° angle in opposite directions.

NOTE: For a half-trapezoid cut the strip the finished width + 1⁄2" x finished length + 7⁄8".

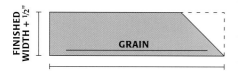

FINISHED LENGTH + 7⁄8"

1. Square up the fabric (page 11). Cut the strip the desired finished width + 1⁄2" (page 12).
2. Reposition the strip horizontally, on or parallel to one of the mat's gridlines.
3. Trim off the uneven edges to square up the end.
4. Cut a rectangle the desired finished length + 1¼".

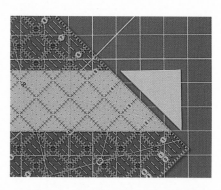

5. Position the ruler, aligning the 45° line on the ruler with the horizontal edge of the rectangle as shown.
6. Cut a 45° angle from exactly the bottom corner to the top edge.

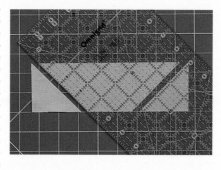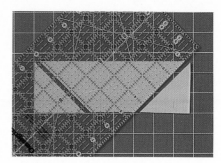

7. Turn the shape by rotating the rotary mat or the fabric shape 180°.
8. Align the 45° line on the ruler to the edge of the fabric as shown and cut.

CUTTING ISOSCELES TRIANGLES IN A SQUARE

MAGIC NUMBERS

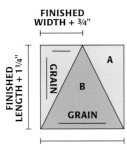

An isosceles triangle in a square is a fairly simple shape to cut. Keep in mind that background A has two sides: a left- and a right-hand side (mirror image). You must always cut the background in double layers, like sides together. This will achieve the mirror imaged shape.

MAGIC NUMBERS

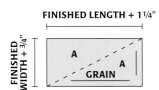

BACKGROUND A

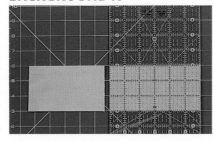 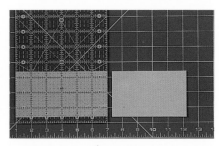

1. Square up the fabric (page 11). Cut one strip the finished width + ¾" (page 12).

2. Reposition the strip horizontally, on or parallel to one of the mat's gridlines.

3. Trim off the uneven edges to square up the end.

4. Open the strip so there are two layers of fabric, *like sides together*, and cut once to get two rectangles the finished length + 1¼".

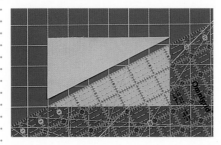 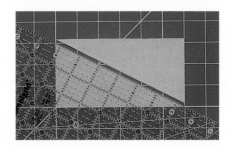

5. Cut the rectangles in half diagonally. This will give you two each of the left- and right-hand backgrounds.

16

MAGIC NUMBER

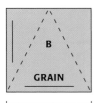

FINISHED SIZE + 7⁄8"

TRIANGLE B

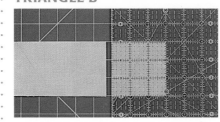 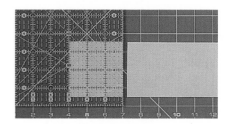

1. Square up the fabric (page 11). Cut one strip the finished size + 7⁄8" (page 12).

2. Reposition the strip horizontally, on or parallel to one of the mat's gridlines.

3. Trim off the uneven edges to square up the end.

4. Cut a square the finished size + 7⁄8".

If all your B triangles are from the same fabric, cut a strip the finished size + 7⁄8". Measure and mark the finished length + 7⁄8" of the first triangle. Fold this length in half to find the top point. Then cut as shown.

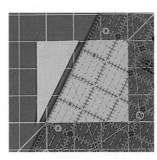 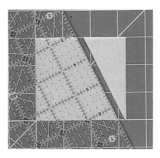

5. Fold the square in half to find the top center and cut from the bottom corner to the top center.

MAGIC NUMBERS

FINISHED SIZE + 7⁄8"

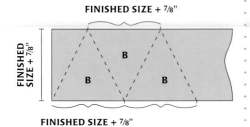

FINISHED SIZE + 7⁄8"

 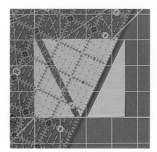

6. Turn the shape by rotating the rotary mat or the fabric shape. This allows you to cover the shape with the ruler when making the cut (see page 10).

7. Cut from the center to the corner.

CUTTING
EQUILATERAL
TRIANGLES

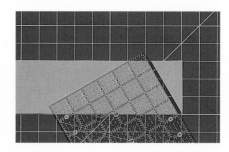
MAGIC NUMBER

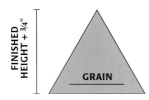

All three sides of an equilateral triangle are equal in length. This triangle starts with a strip. To achieve this cut you will use the 60° markings on your ruler. When working with equilateral triangles, measure the distance between the top and the base and add ¾". This is unlike the previous measurements we have taken, for which we measured the edge of the shape.

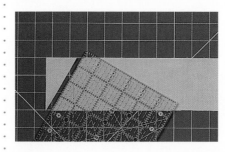
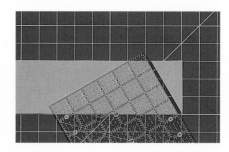

1. Square up the fabric (page 11). Cut the strip the desired finished height + ¾" (page 12).

2. Reposition the strip horizontally, on or parallel to one of the mat's gridlines.

3. Trim off the uneven edges to square up the end.

4. For the first 60° cut align the 60° line on the ruler with the horizontal edge of the strip as shown.

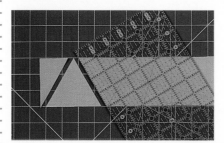
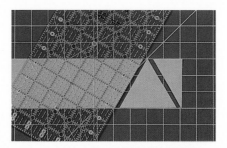

5. Rotate the ruler so now the other 60° line is aligned with the edge of the strip. Notice that the finished shape is not always covered by the ruler. For more complicated shapes like this one it is more practical to rotate the ruler, leaving the finished shape unprotected, than to rotate the rotary mat or fabric shape each time you cut.

6. Cut.

Make sure the measurement of the triangle from the top to the bottom is the measurement of the initial cut strip. If your 60° cut is off, the error will show up here.

CUTTING DIAMONDS

MAGIC NUMBER

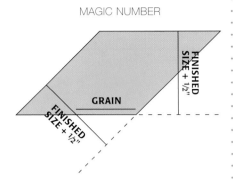

Diamonds also start with a strip. Measure the distance between the two sets of parallel lines and add ½". This, like the equilateral triangle, is unlike the previous measurements we have taken, for which we measured the edge of the shape. To achieve this cut you will use the 45° lines on your ruler.

NOTE: If the diamond is elongated, the pieced unit will have a left and a right side (mirror image). Cut a strip the finished width plus ½" by the full width of the fabric. Fold the strip lengthwise, like sides together, aligning the edges perfectly, and cut at a 45° angle. Move the ruler to make the appropriate second cut.

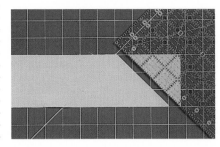 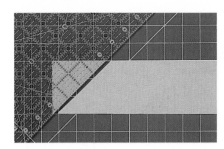

1. Square up the fabric (page 11). Cut the strip the desired finished width + ½" (page 12).

2. Reposition the strip horizontally, on or parallel to one of the mat's gridlines.

3. Trim off the uneven edges to square up the end.

4. Position the ruler, aligning the 45° line with the horizontal edge of the strip as shown. Make the first 45° cut.

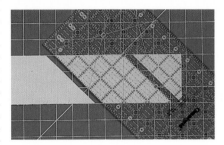 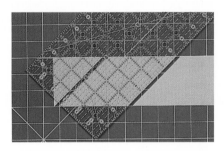

5. Slide your ruler across the cut strip to the appropriate measurement, keeping the 45° line aligned with the edge of the strip. Remember you are measuring the width between the parallel lines.

6. Cut.

Magic Numbers
Quick Reference Guide

These measurements will be the sizes to cut your shapes with seam allowances included.

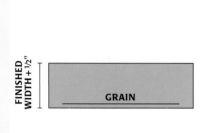

Strip
MAGIC NUMBER

90°
GRAIN

FINISHED SIZE +1¼"

Quarter-Square Triangle
MAGIC NUMBER

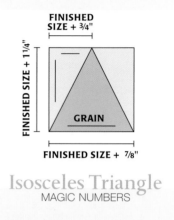

FINISHED SIZE + ¾"

FINISHED SIZE + 1¼"

GRAIN

FINISHED SIZE + ⅞"

Isosceles Triangle
MAGIC NUMBERS

GRAIN

FINISHED SIZE + ½"

Square & Rectangle
MAGIC NUMBER

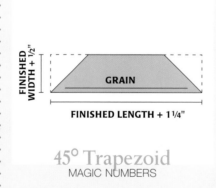

FINISHED WIDTH + ½"

GRAIN

FINISHED LENGTH + 1¼"

45° Trapezoid
MAGIC NUMBERS

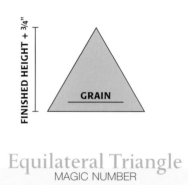

FINISHED HEIGHT + ¾"

GRAIN

Equilateral Triangle
MAGIC NUMBER

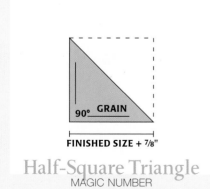

90° GRAIN

FINISHED SIZE + ⅞"

Half-Square Triangle
MAGIC NUMBER

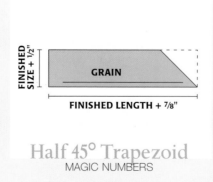

FINISHED SIZE + ½"

GRAIN

FINISHED LENGTH + ⅞"

Half 45° Trapezoid
MAGIC NUMBERS

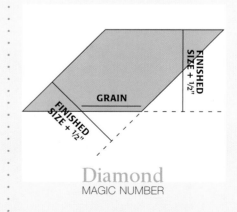

FINISHED SIZE + ½"

FINISHED SIZE + ½"

GRAIN

Diamond
MAGIC NUMBER

Some Basics

STITCHING

Set the stitch length on your machine just long enough so your seam ripper slides nicely in under the stitch. Backtacking is not necessary if the seam ends will be enclosed by other seams. Use a ¼" seam allowance unless otherwise noted.

PRESSING

The arrows on the illustrations indicate which way to press the seams. Pressing seams in one direction or another has to do with ease of construction, not the color value of the fabric. If more than six seams converge in one area, sometimes I press the seams open. This helps avoid large lumps that are unsightly and difficult to quilt through.

Many of the shapes in this book have multiple bias edges. To avoid the stretching of these edges pressing becomes an extremely important issue. Here are some habits you need to develop:

1. Press on a firm surface. An ironing board with a single pad and cover is fine.

2. Press your fabric before cutting it. Remember to use spray starch or sizing when preparing the fabric for the first cut if it seems to lack body.

3. Once you have cut the shape, never press unless you are

moving the seams to one side or the other. Random pressing can inadvertently stretch exposed bias edges.

4. When pressing the seams to one side press the pieced units from the right side of the fabric. This helps avoid pressing tucks into the sewn seams.

5. When pressing seams open, press from the wrong side of the fabric, using your fingernail to gently open the seam as you approach it with the iron.

6. If possible, always approach the pieced unit with the iron on the side of the shape that has the straight of grain. Avoid touching any exposed bias edges with the iron.

While these tips might seem trite or picky, developing these habits can make or break your quilt. A little bit of caution goes a long way when working with unusual shapes.

PINNING

I like to pin. I know that half of the quilting world squirms at this proclamation. But for the little time it takes, the results are well worth it. With basic strip piecing, when no seams have to line up, it is often not necessary to pin. But as you learn more complicated blocks pinning is the only way to assure accuracy. Here is how I pin:

1. Use only extra-fine, glass head pins. They do cost more, but the less expensive "quilting" pins are thick and long. They will distort seam alignments.

2. When aligning two seams that are pressed in opposite directions, place a pin no more than ⅛" on each side of the seam.

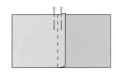

Pin aligned seams

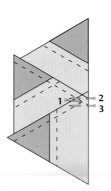

Place pins 2 and 3 on each side of pin 1

3. If you have two pieces that need to align exactly, insert the first pin (pin 1) from the wrong side of the pieced unit on the top (exactly at the intersection), into the right side of the pieced unit underneath (exactly at the other intersection). Push the head of the pin tightly into the fabric. While holding this pin firmly in place, secure pins 2 and 3 on each side of pin 1, no more than ⅛" on each side. As you approach the intersection while sewing the seam, remove pin 1 at the last second so your sewing machine needle can go into the hole created by pin 1. It works!

SEAM RIPPING

On occasion you might need to pick out a seam. Please use a seam ripper with a sharp blade. Inexpensive, dull rippers can stretch or ruin the fabric and will cause you nothing but heartache. To pick out a seam, cut every third thread on one side of the pieced unit, then gently lift the thread off the other side of the fabric. Your stitch length should be just long enough that the ripper can nicely slide right under the stitch.

If you have two bias edges sewn together, seriously consider throwing the pieces out and starting over rather than ripping out the seam. The chance of stretching the bias edges is almost 100%. If the edges do stretch, the shapes won't align or sew together properly.

SETS

There are two different types of sets used in this book. A set refers to the way the blocks are laid out and sewn before the borders are attached.

A straight set is when the blocks are positioned with the sides parallel to the quilt's edge.

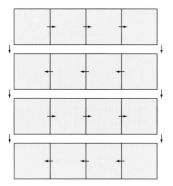

Straight set pressing

Once the blocks are sewn into rows it is best to press the seams of each row in alternating directions (e.g. row 1 right, row 2 left, etc.). This will allow you to easily align the seams when sewing the rows together. After the rows are sewn together, press the seams in one direction.

A diagonal set is when the blocks are set on point and sewn in rows on the diagonal.

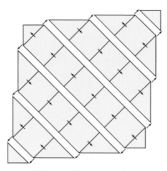

Diagonal set pressing

BORDERS

Borders are simply strips. However, if the length of the border is longer than the regular width of fabric (42"), it will become necessary to cut the borders on the fabric's lengthwise grain. When following project instructions it is wise to cut the borders first, because before you know it the length of the fabric becomes too short from cutting strips for various pieces in the quilt. When pre-cutting the border strips always add a few inches for insurance.

To determine the exact length of the border strips measure your sewn quilt top across the center from top to bottom and from side to side. Compare your measurements against the project instructions and if necessary adjust the cutting measurements of the border strips to the actual length and width of your quilt top.

BACKING

Once you have finished your quilt top it's time to consider the backing. Most of the projects in this book are wider than the standard 42"-wide 100% cotton, so it will be necessary to piece the backing. I often use fabric I wonder why I ever bought (in colors that relate to the quilt) or the focus fabric that wasn't used up. When preparing the backing here are thoughts to keep in mind:

1. It's OK to use more than one fabric on the pieced back.

2. Never use a sheet or designer fabric. It has a higher thread count and is difficult to hand quilt through.

3. Always cut off the selvage edge before piecing the fabrics together, as it is difficult to hand quilt through and the seam might not lay flat.

4. If your quilt top has a lot of white in it, use a light-colored fabric on the back. A darker fabric could show through, distorting the colors and the look of the pieced top.

5. Always prewash the backing fabric and piece it a few inches larger on each side than the quilt top, since it can shift during the quilting process. After the quilting is finished, then you can trim the batting and backing to the exact size of the pieced quilt top.

BATTING

For hand quilting I recommend starting with a low-loft polyester batting. It makes the quilting stitch much easier to learn.

For machine quilting I recommend you use a 100% cotton batting. Make sure you follow the instructions if it needs to be prewashed.

LAYERING

Depending on the size of my project, I either work on a table top (small quilt) or on my non-loop carpet (large quilt). First you must either tape down the backing (table top) or pin using T pins (carpet). It should be wrong side up. Get it taut. No bubbles or ripples are acceptable, as they will result in folds and tucks on the back of your finished quilt.

Carefully unroll the batting and smooth it on top of the backing. Trim the batting to the same size as the backing. Smooth the quilt top over the batting right side up. Pin the edges of the quilt top to the batting and backing to prevent shifting while you baste.

BASTING

FOR HAND QUILTING

Knot one end of a neutral-colored thread and take large stitches through all three layers.

Don't bother knotting the other end of the thread. When it's time to remove the basting you can just give the knotted end of the thread a little tug and it will pull out.

I like to baste in an approximately 4" grid pattern, so there is an even amount of basting throughout the quilt. Never skimp on this part of the process. It will only cause disaster down the road, since your quilt layers may slip and move during the quilting process.

FOR MACHINE QUILTING

Unlike what you would do for hand quilting, you will pin baste every 3" with small safety pins. Pin evenly across the quilt, avoiding areas where the quilting stitches will be sewn.

QUILTING

I love to hand quilt but unfortunately, I do not always have the time for it. I determine how the quilt will be used and then decide how to handle the quilting process. But for either hand quilting or machine quilting I have three thoughts to share with you:

1. More is better. Never skimp on the amount of quilting on your quilt.

2. Treat the pieced surface as a whole. I rarely quilt ¼" from the seamlines because it throws the most unsightly part of the quilt (the seams) right up into your eyes. Therefore, you will often find that my quilts are quilted with interesting grids.

3. Use an equal amount of quilting over the entire surface. If you quilt different areas with uneven density your quilt will not only look odd, but it will also sag and not lay flat.

BINDING

1. Trim the batting and backing even with the edges of the quilt top.

2. Your new-found skill of strip cutting will come in handy when it is time to cut the binding. Cut the strips selvage to selvage. I usually cut my binding strips 2⅛" wide. If it is necessary to piece it to make it longer, I like to use a diagonal seam. To achieve this follow the illustrations.

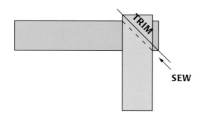

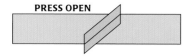

Piece the binding strips. Trim the seams.

3. Trim two strips to the width of the quilt from side to side + 1".

4. Fold and press lengthwise.

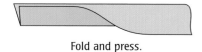

Fold and press.

5. On the top edge of the quilt, align the raw edges of the binding with the raw edge of the quilt. Let the binding extend ½" past the corners of the quilt. Sew using a ¼" seam allowance. Repeat for the bottom edge of the quilt.

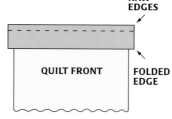

Attach binding to front of quilt.

6. Bring the folded edge of the binding over the raw edges of the quilt and slip stitch to the back of the quilt. Trim the ends even with the quilt.

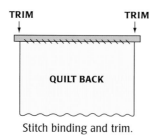

Stitch binding and trim.

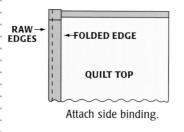

Attach side binding.

7. For the two sides of the quilt cut the binding the length of the quilt + ½" for turning under. Fold over the two ends of the binding to create a finished edge and sew onto the quilt. Again turn the folded edge of the binding over the the raw edge of the quilt and slip stitch into place.

Voila! With the addition of a fabric label on the back documenting your effort, your quilt is finished.

Melon Ball

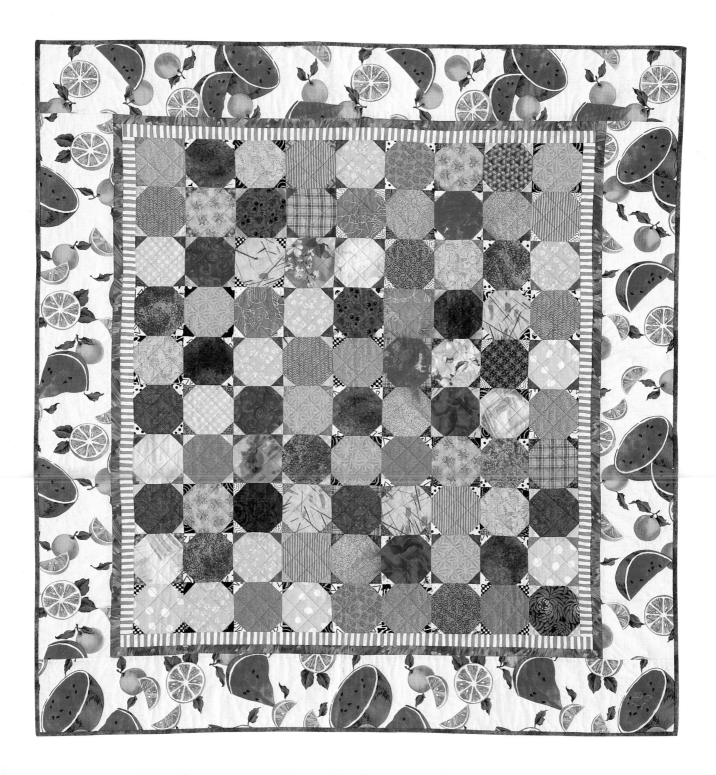

This quilt measures 50½" x 54½" and is comprised of strips and squares.
It is made of ninety 4" finished melon balls. Machine quilted by Paula Reid.

I fell in love with this watermelon and orange fabric, perfect for a melon ball quilt. For the blocks I decided to use a lot of the "hot" colors that are available today. The black-and-white geometric prints in the little corners of many of the blocks offer a place for the eyes to rest. To calm this vivacious quilt the first striped inner border holds the blocks together visually. This quilt was so much fun to make because of the simplicity of the block and the playfulness of the fabric. This quilt really appeals to my teenage friends.

Fabric
Requirements

(Fabric requirements are based on 42" fabric width.) Feel free to use a wider variety of fabrics, but remember to adjust the number of squares cut from each strip.

Melon balls and background corners: ¼ yard each of ten fabrics (yellow, orange, red, and green)

Background corners: ⅛ yard each of three fabrics (black-and-white geometric prints)

Inner borders: ¼ yard each of two fabrics

Outer border: 1½ yards

Backing: 3 yards

Binding: ⅜ yard

Batting: 54" x 58"

MELON BALL BLOCK

Cutting

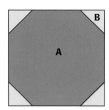

Melon Ball block

Please refer to the rotary cutting instructions beginning on page 9 for guidance.

A SQUARES

◆ Cut one 4½" x 42" strip from each of the ten melon ball fabrics.

◆ Cut nine 4½" squares from each strip (90 total).

B SQUARES

◆ Cut one 1½" x 42" strip from each of the ten melon ball fabrics for background corners.

◆ Cut twenty-eight 1½" squares from each strip (280 total).

◆ Cut one 1½" x 42" strip from each of the three black-and-white geometric fabrics for the background corners.

◆ Cut twenty-eight 1½" squares from each strip (need only 80 total).

Block Construction

Use ¼" seam allowance. Press following the arrows.

1. Draw a line diagonally, corner to corner, on the wrong side of the 1½" squares.

Draw a line corner to corner.

2. Place the four 1½" squares in the four corners of one of the 4½" squares, right sides together, as shown.

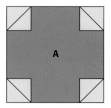

Place 1½" squares in corners of 4½" square.

3. Sew directly on the drawn line and trim.

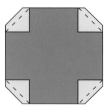

Sew on drawn line and trim.

4. Press following the arrows.

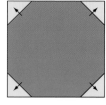

Press

5. Repeat to make 90 Melon Ball blocks.

QUILT TOP CONSTRUCTION

1. Arrange your blocks in a pleasing manner in a straight set.

2. Sew each row, press, then sew all the rows together. Press.

Your quilt top should measure 36½" x 40½". If it does, use the instructions below to cut and attach the inner and outer border strips. If it doesn't, see page 22 to measure and cut the correct border lengths for your quilt top.

First Inner Border

1. Cut two 1½" x 40½" strips. Sew onto each side. Press toward the inner border.

2. Cut two 1½" x 38½" strips. Sew onto the top and bottom. Press toward the inner border.

Second Inner Border

1. Cut two 1¼" x 42½" strips. Sew onto each side. Press toward the second inner border.

2. Cut two 1¼" x 40" strips. Sew onto the top and bottom. Press toward the second inner border.

Outer Border

1. Cut two 6" x 44" strips lengthwise. Sew onto each side. Press.

2. Cut two 6" x 51" strips lengthwise. Sew onto the top and bottom. Press.

3. Layer, baste, and quilt as desired.

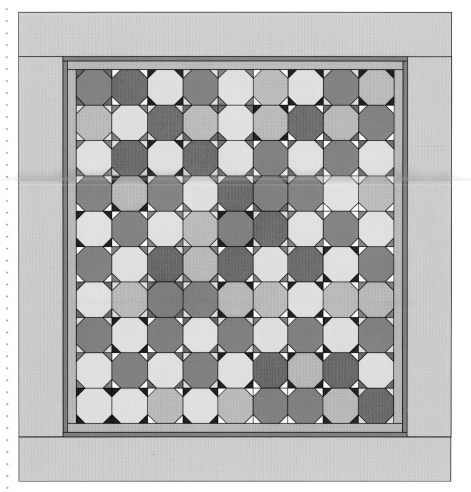

Quilt construction

Nine-Patch Variation

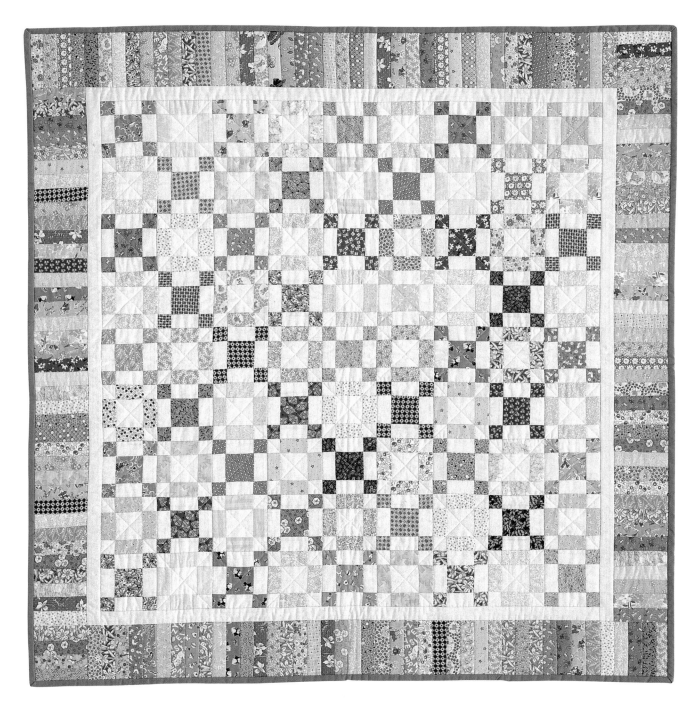

This quilt measures 46½" x 46½" and is comprised of strips, squares, and rectangles. It is made of eighty-one 4" finished nine-patches. Machine quilted by Paula Reid.

I didn't think I was particularly fond of the 1930's reproduction fabrics available today, so I was amazed to find so many in my private collection. Somehow they had sneaked right into my fabric stash. I decided it was time to get familiar with them. Through the process of making this quilt I found myself drawn to the colors and prints indicative of that time period. Upon completion of this little quilt, I found, much to my surprise, that I liked it! It's always rewarding when you take on a color family or use fabric that is outside your personal comfort zone and create with it. You will build your understanding of fabric relationships and become a better quilter for it. The pattern is quite easy and gives charming results.

Fabric
Requirements

(Fabric requirements are based on 42" fabric width.)

A blocks and outer border: ⅛ yard each of eleven 1930s reproduction fabrics (medium to medium dark colors), total of 2½ yards assorted

B blocks and outer border: ⅛ yard each of eleven 1930s reproduction fabrics (light to medium-light colors)

Block background and inner border: 1¼ yards off-white

Backing: 3 yards

Binding: ⅓ yard

Batting: 50" x 50"

NINE-PATCH VARIATION BLOCK

Cutting

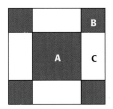

Nine-Patch Block A

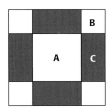

Nine-Patch Block B

Please refer to the rotary cutting instructions beginning on page 9 for guidance. You will need 41 A blocks and 40 B blocks.

BLOCK A

A Squares and B Squares

◈ Cut one 2½" x 42" strip from each of the eleven A block fabrics.

◈ Cut four 2½" squares (A) from each strip (need only 41 total). Then trim the strips to 1½" wide and cut twelve 1½" squares (B) from three strips and sixteen 1½" squares (B) from eight strips (164 total).

C Rectangles

◈ Cut seven 2½" x 42" strips of off-white.

◈ Cut twenty-four 1½" x 2½" rectangles (C) from each strip (need only 164 total).

BLOCK B

A Squares and B Squares

◈ Cut three 2½" x 42" strips of off-white.

◈ Cut sixteen 2½" squares (A) from each strip (need only 40 total).

◈ Cut seven 1½" x 42" strips of off-white.

◈ Cut twenty-three 1½" squares (B) from each strip (need only 160 total).

C Rectangles

◈ Cut one 2½" x 42" strip from each of the eleven B block fabrics.

◈ Cut twelve 1½" x 2½" rectangles (C) from four strips and cut sixteen 1½" x 2½" rectangles (C) from seven strips (160 total).

Block Construction

Use ¼" seam allowance.

Piece and press following the arrows. Make 41 A blocks and 40 B blocks.

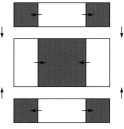

Block A construction

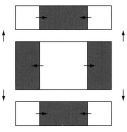

Block B construction

QUILT TOP CONSTRUCTION

1. Arrange your blocks in a pleasing manner in a straight set.

2. Sew each row, press, then sew all the rows together. Press.

Your quilt top should measure 36½" x 36½". If it does, use the instructions below to cut and attach the inner and outer border strips. If it doesn't, see page 22 to measure and cut the correct border lengths for your quilt top. You may need to add or delete rectangles to adjust the outer border to fit your quilt top.

Inner Border

1. Cut two 1½" x 36½" strips. Sew onto the sides. Press toward the inner border.

2. Cut two 1½" x 38½" strips. Sew onto the top and bottom. Press toward the inner border.

Outer Border

1. Cut 168 1½" x 4½" rectangles.

2. Sew thirty-eight rectangles together for each top and bottom border. Sew forty-six rectangles together for each side border. Notice that on one end of each side border four of the

rectangles are turned 90°. Press.

3. Sew the top and bottom border onto the quilt top. Press toward the outer border.

4. Sew on each side border and press toward the outer border.

5. Layer, baste, and quilt as desired.

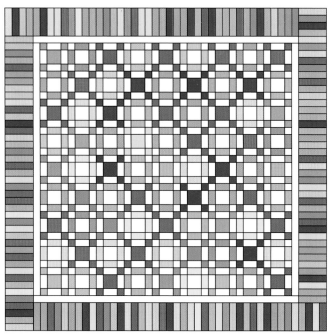

Quilt construction

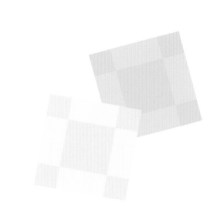

Star of Hope

This quilt measures 34½" x 40½" and is comprised of squares, half-square triangles, and quarter-square triangles. It is made of thirty 6" finished stars. Machine quilted by Paula Reid.

This sea shell fabric really struck me when I saw it in the quilt shop. It had the wonderful new melon color we are seeing more and more, and I liked how the fabric designer mixed the browns and pinks with the melon. Looking for interesting prints, I picked fabrics that related to all the different colors in the shell fabric. This method of fabric selection is called using a focus fabric. You are letting the fabric designer inspire the color selection for you.

Fabric
Requirements

(Fabric requirements are based on 42" fabric width.)

Dark stars and border: 1/8 yard each of ten different browns

Melon star tips and border: 1/8 yard each of six melon fabrics

Background: 1 yard off-white

Alternate squares and border: 1/2 yard focus fabric

Backing: 1 1/4 yard

Binding: 1/4 yard total of assorted browns

Batting: 38" x 44"

STAR OF HOPE BLOCK

Cutting

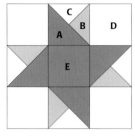
Star of Hope block

Please refer to the rotary cutting instructions beginning on page 9 for guidance.

BROWN STARS

◆ Cut one 2⅞" x 42" strip from each of the ten brown fabrics.

◆ Cut six 2⅞" squares from each strip (60 total), then cut in half diagonally (half-square triangles) (A).

◆ Cut three 2⅞" squares from four strips and two 2⅞" squares from six strips (need only 21 total), then cut in half diagonally (half-square triangles). Set these aside to be used in the border.

◆ Trim the remaining strips to 2½" wide and cut three 2½" squares (E) from each strip (30 total).

MELON STAR TIPS

◆ Cut one 3¼" x 42" strip from each of the six melon fabrics.

◆ Cut five 3¼" squares from each strip (30 total), then cut in half diagonally twice (quarter-square triangles) (B). Set aside the left-over fabric for the border.

BACKGROUND

◆ Cut three 3¼" x 42" strips of off-white.

◆ Cut twelve 3¼" squares from each strip (need only 30 total), then cut in half diagonally twice (quarter-square triangles) (C).

◆ Cut four 2⅞" x 42" strips of off-white.

◆ Cut twelve 2⅞" squares from each strip (need only 40 total), then cut in half diagonally (half-square triangles) (F).

◆ Cut three 2½" x 42" strips.

◆ Cut fourteen 2½" squares (D) from each strip (need only 40 total).

FOCUS FABRIC

◆ Cut two strips 3⅜" x 42" from focus fabric.

◆ Cut eleven 3⅜" squares (G) from each strip (20 total). Set aside leftover fabric for the border.

QUILT TOP CONSTRUCTION

Use ¼" seam allowance. Press following the arrows. Press all seams open where two (C) shapes come together. Accurate stitching is necessary in order for the pieced border to fit.

1. Arrange the star points and squares, background triangles and squares, and focus fabric squares. Use the photo as a guide.

2. Sew together the background and melon quarter-square triangle (B/C) units, then join to the 2⅞" brown triangles (A). Place these units back in the arrangement.

Press following the arrows.

3. Sew the 2½" half-square background triangles (F) to the 3⅜" focus fabric squares (G). Place these units back in the arrangement.

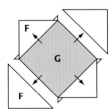

Press following the arrows.

4. Sew the pieces in rows as shown and press following the arrows. Note that each individual star isn't formed until the rows are sewn together. Press.

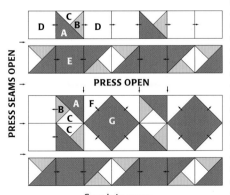

Sew into rows.

Your quilt top should measure 30½" x 36½".

Border

◆ Trim the six leftover melon fabric strips to 2⅞" wide.

◆ Cut three 2⅞" squares from one strip and two 2⅞" squares from five strips (13 total), then cut in half diagonally (half-square triangles).

◆ Gather the brown half-square triangles that were set aside to be used for the border.

◆ Cut three 2⅞" x 42" strips of focus fabric.

◆ Cut twelve 2⅞" squares from each strip (need only 34 total), then cut in half diagonally (half-square triangles).

◆ Trim one of these remaining strips to 2½" wide and cut two 2½" squares.

1. Pair a focus fabric triangle with each brown and melon triangle and stitch to form sixty-four border squares.

2. Arrange in a pleasing manner around the quilt.

3. Stitch eighteen border squares together and add to one of the sides of the quilt top. Repeat for the other side.

4. Stitch sixteen border squares together. Add a 2½" focus fabric square to one end. Add to the top edge of the quilt top with the square on the left. Repeat for the bottom border, with the square on the right.

5. Layer, baste, and quilt as desired.

Quilt construction

33

Houses and Trees

This quilt measures 45½" x 47½" and is comprised of strips, squares, rectangles, 45° trapezoids, and isosceles triangles. It is made of thirty 4" x 6" finished trees and twelve 6" finished houses. Machine quilted by Paula Reid.

I wanted this quilt to have a country look, so I sought out fabric that had a lot of brown, gold, red, and blue. What surprised me about this fabric is that the blue was teal. I thought this was a rather unusual choice for an autumn color palette, which is why I liked it. To keep the country look I decided not to use any fabric with a lot of white in it. That gave the quilt its snuggle-up warm feeling.

Fabric
Requirements

(Fabric requirements are based on 42" fabric width.) Feel free to use a wider variety of fabrics, but remember to adjust the number of shapes cut from each strip.

Houses: ¼ yard each of five different blues

Roofs: ⅛ yard each of three different reds

Doors and windows: ⅛ yard each of two different yellows

Trees: ¼ yard each of five different greens

Tree trunks: ⅛ yard each of two different browns

Background: ⅛ yard each of nine light fabrics

Inner border: ¼ yard

Outer border: 1⅓ yards

Backing: 3 yards

Binding: ⅓ yard of assorted reds

Batting: 49" x 51"

HOUSE BLOCKS

Cutting

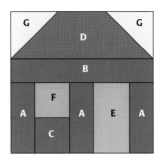
House block

Please refer to the rotary cutting instructions beginning on page 9 for guidance.

HOUSE FRONTS

◆ Cut one 1½" x 42" and one 2" x 42" strip from each of the five blue fabrics.

C Squares

◆ Cut three 2" squares (need only 12 total) from each of the 2" wide strips. Then trim the remainder of the strips to 1½" wide.

A Rectangles and B Rectangles

◆ Cut eight 1½" x 3½" (need only 36 total) rectangles (A) and three 1½" x 6½" (need only 12 total) rectangles (B) from each strip.

ROOFS

D Trapezoids

◆ Cut one 2½" x 42 strip from each of the three red fabrics.

◆ Cut four 2½" x 7¼" rectangles from each strip (12 total), then trim off each end of the rectangles at a 45° angle (45° trapezoids).

DOORS AND WINDOWS

E Rectangles and F Squares

◆ Cut one 2" x 42" strip from each of the two yellow fabrics.

◆ Cut seven 2" x 3½" rectangles (E) and seven 2" squares (F) from each strip (need only 12 total of each shape).

BACKGROUND

G Squares

◆ Cut one 2⅞" x 42" strip from one of the light fabrics.

◆ Cut twelve 2⅞" squares, then cut in half diagonally (half-square triangles).

Block Construction

Use ¼" seam allowance. Press following the arrows.

The ^ indicates which edge or point to line up. Piece and press following the arrows as shown. Make 12 House blocks.

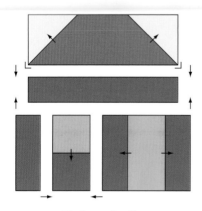
Block construction

TREE BLOCKS

Cutting

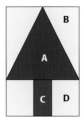

Tree block

Please refer to the rotary cutting instructions beginning on page 9 for guidance.

TREE TOPS

A Triangles

◆ Cut one 4⅞" x 42" strip from each of the five green fabrics.

◆ Cut six 4⅞" squares from each strip (30 total), then cut isosceles triangles from these squares (isosceles triangle in a square).

TREE TRUNKS

C Rectangles

◆ Cut one 2½" x 42" strip from each of the two brown fabrics.

◆ Cut fifteen 1½" x 2½" rectangles (30 total).

BACKGROUND

B Triangles

◆ Cut one 2¾" x 42" strip from each of the remaining eight light fabrics. *Important:* Keep the strips folded right sides together selvage to selvage—the background is a mirror image.

◆ Cut four 2¾" x 5¼" rectangles from each strip (need only 30 total).

Cut the rectangles in half diagonally. Each two-layer rectangle will give background triangles for two trees.

D Rectangles

◆ Trim the leftover strips from above to 2½" wide.

◆ Cut eight 2" x 2½" rectangles from each strip (need 60 total).

Block Construction

Use ¼" seam allowance. Press following the arrows.

The ∧ indicates which edge or point to line up. Piece and press as shown. Make 30 Tree blocks.

LINE UP INNER POINTS

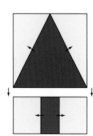

Block construction

QUILT TOP CONSTRUCTION

1. Arrange your blocks in a pleasing manner in a straight set.

2. Sew each row, then sew all the rows together. Press.

Your quilt top should measure 32½" x 36½". If it does, use the instructions below to cut and attach the inner and outer border strips. If it doesn't, see page 22 to measure and cut the correct border lengths for your quilt top.

Inner Border

1. Cut two 1½" x 36½" strips. Sew onto each side. Press toward the inner border.

2. Cut two 1½" x 34½" strips. Sew onto the top and bottom. Press toward the inner border.

Outer Border

1. Cut two 6" x 34½" strips. Sew onto the top and bottom. Press toward the outer border.

2. Cut two 6" x 47½" strips. Sew onto each side and press toward the outer border.

3. Layer, baste, and quilt as desired.

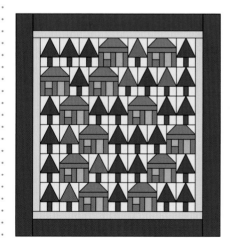

Quilt construction

Baskets and Nine-Patches

This quilt measures 48½" x 48½" and is comprised of strips, squares, half-square triangles, quarter-square triangles, and diamonds. It is made of sixteen 6" finished baskets and nine 6" finished nine-patches. Machine quilted by Paula Reid.

Being an almost-native Californian I am naturally drawn to poppies. When I saw this fabric I knew it was perfect for my basket quilt. For the flowers in the baskets I randomly cut diamonds and didn't give much thought to choosing which color diamonds ended up in each basket. I approached this quilt how Mother Nature creates a wildflower field, giving a random and joyful look.

Fabric
Requirements

(Fabric requirements are based on 42" fabric width.) Feel free to use a wider variety of fabrics, but remember to adjust the number of shapes cut from each strip.

Nine-patches, setting triangles and outer border: 2⅛ yards floral

Background: ¾ yard white

Baskets: ⅛ yard each of three different greens

Diamonds: ⅛ yard each of six fabrics

Alternate nine-patches: ⅓ yard pink

Inner border: ¼ yard blue

Backing: 3 yards

Binding: ⅓ yard blue stripe

Batting: 52" x 52"

BASKET BLOCKS

Cutting

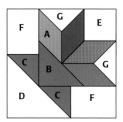
Basket block

Please refer to the rotary cutting instructions beginning on page 9 for guidance.

FLOWERS

A Diamonds

◆ Cut one 1¾" x 42" strip from each of the six diamond fabrics.

◆ Cut twelve 1¾" x 1¾" diamonds from each strip (need only 64 total).

BASKETS

B Triangles

◆ Cut one 3⅜" x 42" strip from each of the three green fabrics.

◆ Cut three 3⅜" squares from each strip (need only 8 total), then cut in half diagonally (half-square triangles).

C Triangles

◆ Trim the remaining strips from above to 2⅝" wide.

◆ Cut six 2⅝" squares from each strip (need only 16 total), then cut in half diagonally (half-square triangles).

BACKGROUND

D Triangle

◆ Cut one 4⅜" x 42" strip of white.

◆ Cut eight 4⅜" squares from the strip, then cut in half diagonally (16 total half-square triangles).

E Squares and F Rectangles

◆ Cut four 2¼" x 42" strips of white.

◆ Cut sixteen 2¼" squares from one strip and eleven 2¼" x 3" rectangles from three strips (need only 32 total).

G Triangles

◆ Cut one 3¾" x 42" strip of white.

◆ Cut eight 3¾" squares, then cut in half diagonally twice (32 total quarter-square triangles).

Block Construction

Use ¼" seam allowance. Press following the arrows.

Mark a dot ¼" in from the 90° corner on the wrong side of the background quarter-square triangle and on the corner square fabrics. This is your stop/start point for the Y seam.

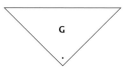
Mark a dot.

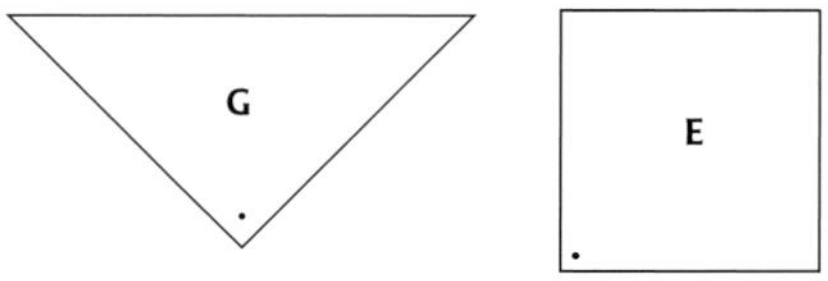

Follow the diagram for piecing sequence. The ∧ indicates what edge or point to line up. Piece the following units as shown.

The arrows indicate which way to press. Only press when indicated.

1. Piece unit A. Sew in the directions the arrows indicate. Stop and backstitch at the dot.

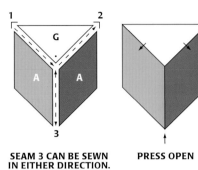

SEAM 3 CAN BE SEWN IN EITHER DIRECTION.   **PRESS OPEN**

2. Press seam A/G following the arrows. Press seam A/A open. Repeat for a second A unit.

3. Piece together the two A units. Sew in the directions the arrows indicate. Stop and backstitch at the dot.

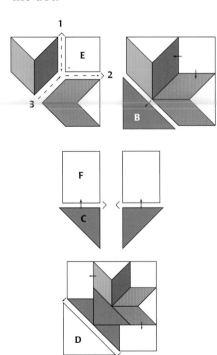

Block construction

4. Continue construction as shown.

5. Repeat to make 16 Basket blocks.

NINE-PATCH BLOCKS

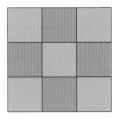

Nine-Patch block

Cutting

◆ Cut five 2½" x 42" strips of floral.

◆ Cut four 2½" x 42" strips of pink.

Block Construction

1. Set A: Sew a floral strip to each side of a pink strip. Press. Repeat to make a second set.

2. Cut Set A into eighteen 2½" segments (using the same technique as for cutting strips).

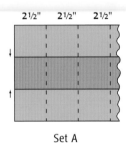

Set A

3. Set B: Sew a pink strip in to each side of a floral strip. Press.

4. Cut Set B into nine 2½" segments.

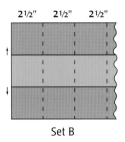

Set B

5. Arrange and sew Sets A and B as shown into nine Nine-Patch blocks. Press.

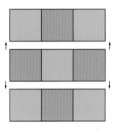

Block construction

SIDE TRIANGLES

You will need a total of twelve quarter-square triangles for the sides and four half-square triangles for the corners.

Cutting

◆ Cut one 9¾" x 42" strip of floral fabric.

◆ Cut three 9¾" squares from this strip, then cut in half diagonally twice (quarter-square triangles) for side triangles.

◆ Cut one 5⅛" strip of floral fabric.

◆ Cut two 5⅛" squares from this strip, then cut in half diagonally (half-square triangles) for corner triangles.

QUILT TOP CONSTRUCTION

1. Arrange your blocks in a pleasing manner in a diagonal set.

2. Join the pieced blocks and the side and corner triangles in a diagonal set.

3. Sew each row. Press. Sew all the rows together. Press.

Your quilt top should measure 34½" x 34½". If it does, use the instructions below to cut and attach the inner and outer border strips. If it doesn't, see page 22 to measure and cut the correct border lengths for your quilt top.

Inner Border

1. Cut two 2" x 34½" strips. Sew onto the top and bottom of the quilt. Press toward the inner border.

2. Cut two 2" x 37½" strips. Sew onto the sides. Press toward the inner border.

Outer Border

1. Cut two 6" x 37½" strips. Sew onto the top and bottom. Press toward the outer border.

2. Cut two 6" x 48½" strips. Sew onto both sides. Press toward the outer border.

3. Layer, baste, and quilt as desired.

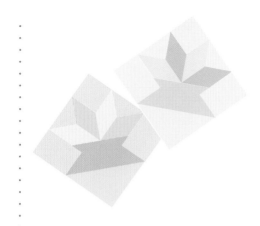

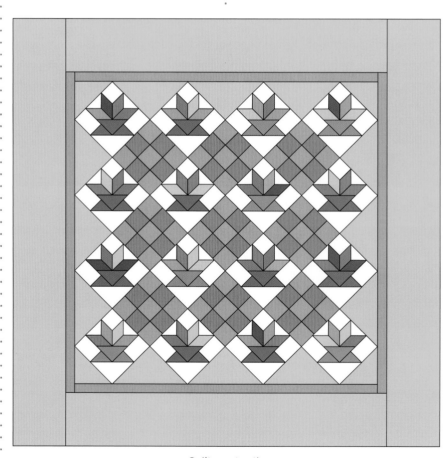

Quilt construction

Whirligig

This quilt measures 51½" x 56½" and is comprised of strips and equilateral triangles.
It is made of thirty-two 6" x 7" finished whirligigs and six half-whirligigs.
Machine quilted by Paula Reid.

Solid-color quilts are always striking, and often provide a great canvas for wonderful quilting designs. I usually reserve solid fabric quilts for easy patterns since every piecing mistake will show. Believe it or not this block is a snap to piece, perfect for this fabric family choice. The unexpected striped inner border adds pizazz to the quilt, making it unique and crisp.

Fabric
Requirements

(Fabric requirements are based on 42" fabric width.)

Whirligigs: ⅛ yard each of twenty-two different solids

Background and outer border: 4½ yards black

Inner border: ¼ yard stripe

Inner border: ¼ yard red

Backing: 3½ yards

Binding: ½ yard of assorted black prints

Batting: 54" x 60"

Note: You will also need spray starch.

WHIRLIGIG BLOCKS

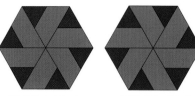

Whirligig Block   Whirligig Block Optional Rotation

Cutting

Please refer to the rotary cutting instructions beginning on page 9 for guidance.

◆ Cut thirty-two 2⅛" x 42" strips of black.

◆ Cut two 2⅛" x 42" strips from sixteen of the solid-colored fabrics.

Block Construction

Use ¼" seam allowance.

1. Sew a black strip to a solid-colored strip lengthwise.

Sew strips together lengthwise.

2. Spray starch heavily and press seam toward the black fabric.

(This step is very important because two sides of the cut triangle will be exposed bias edges. The spray starch will help prevent the bias from stretching).

3. Cut the strip into equilateral triangles. You will have two sets of six each. We will be using the set with the black triangle. Save the other set to play with for another quilt with a completely different look.

Six from each strip   Six extra

Note: To create the random playful spirit of this quilt the pieced equilateral triangles are rotated in two different directions. At first I identified this as a mistake, but after re-piecing the units I decided I liked it better a little random. This was the classic case of making lemonade from lemons!

4. Piece and press as shown. Remember to be extremely careful when pressing. Unfortunately your iron will have to pass over some exposed bias edges.

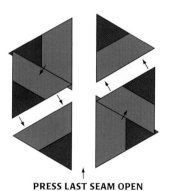

PRESS LAST SEAM OPEN

Block construction

5. As you complete each block immediately stitch around ⅛" in from the raw edge. This will help secure the exposed bias edges until the blocks are sewn into a complete quilt top.

Stitch ⅛" around block.

HALF-WHIRLIGIG BLOCK

Cutting

◆ Cut three 2⅛" x 42" strips of black. Cut in half to measure 2⅛" x 21".

◆ Cut one 2⅛" x 42" strip of each of the remaining six solid-colored fabrics. Cut in half to measure 2⅛" x 21".

Block Construction

1. Prepare as in Steps 1 and 2 on page 42.

2. Cut four equilateral triangles from each strip set.

3. Piece and press following the arrows as shown.

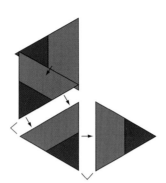

Block construction

Background Triangles

◆ Cut six 3¾" x 42" strips of black.

◆ Cut seventy-eight equilateral triangles from the strips.

QUILT TOP CONSTRUCTION

1. Lay out the blocks in a pleasing manner. The odd rows start and end with a whole Whirligig block. The even rows start and end with a Half-whirligig block.

2. Sew the blocks together in rows using the black triangles as the background. Press seams open.

Sew in rows.

3. Sew all the rows together and press seams open. Trim the ragged edges allowing for ¼" seam allowance.

Sew the rows together and trim.

43

In a perfect world your quilt top should measure 35½" x 42½". If it does, use the instructions here to cut and attach the inner and outer border strips. But because many of the Whirligig block's outside edges are exposed bias, distortion can occur so there's a good chance it will not measure the above size. See page 22 to measure and cut the correct border lengths.

Striped Inner Border

1. Cut two 2" x 42½" strips. Sew onto each side. Press toward the inner border.

2. Cut two 2" x 38½" strips. Sew onto the top and bottom. Press toward the inner border.

Red Inner Border

1. Cut two 1½" x 45½" strips. Sew onto each side. Press toward the red border.

2. Cut two 1½" x 40½" strips. Sew onto the top and bottom and press toward the red border.

Black Outer Border

1. Cut two 6" x 45½" strips. Sew onto each side and press toward the outer border.

2. Cut two 6" x 51½" strips. Sew onto the top and bottom and press toward the outer border.

3. Layer, baste, and quilt as desired.

Quilt construction

Sampler

This sampler quilt measures 36½" x 46¼" and shows how a variety of blocks can be used in one quilt. Machine quilted by Paula Reid.

This particular sampler is a wonderful exploration of rotary cutting combined with fabric fun. I simply chose a fabulous piece of focus fabric for the border and then let the play begin, using my stash of fabric. I encourage you to try all the blocks. You will be surprised just how easy it really is!

To complete the quilt pictured you will need to make:

◆ 12 Melon Ball blocks (4" finished)

◆ 3 Nine-Patch Variation blocks (4" finished)

◆ 4 Star of Hope blocks (6" finished)

◆ 4 House blocks (6" finished)

◆ 4 Tree blocks (4" x 6" finished)

◆ 4 Basket blocks (6" finished)

◆ 4 Whirligig blocks (6" x 7" finished)

Fabric
Requirements

(Fabric requirements are based on 42" fabric width.)

Blocks: assorted fabrics

Inner border: ¼ yard

Outer border: ¾ yard

Backing: 1¼ yard

Binding: ⅜ yard

Batting: 43" x 47"

Cutting

Cutting instructions are given for one block. Use ¼" seam allowance.

MELON BALL

◆ One 4½" square (A).

◆ Four 1½" squares (B).

See page 26 for more detailed instructions.

NINE-PATCH VARIATION

Block A

◆ One 2½" square (A).

◆ Four 1½" squares (B).

◆ Four 1½" x 2½" rectangles (C).

Block B

◆ One 2½" square (A).

◆ Four 1½" square (B).

◆ Four 1½" x 2½" rectangles (C).

See page 29 for more detailed instructions.

STAR OF HOPE VARIATION

Star

◆ One 2½" square (E).

◆ Two 2⅞" squares, then cut in half diagonally (A).

Small star tip

◆ One 3¼" square, then cut in half diagonally twice (quarter-square triangles) (B).

Background

◆ One 3¼" square, then cut in half diagonally twice (quarter-square triangles) (C).

◆ Four 2½" squares (D).

See page 32 for more detailed instructions.

HOUSE

House front

◆ Three 1½" x 3½" rectangles (A).

◆ One 1½" x 6½" rectangle (B).

◆ One 2" square (C).

Roof

◆ One 2½" x 7¼" rectangle, then cut off each end at a 45° angle (trapezoid) (D).

Door and window

◆ One 2" x 3½" rectangle (E).

◆ One 2" square (F).

Background

◆ One 2⅞" square, then cut in half diagonally (half-square triangles) (G).

See page 35 for more detailed instructions.

TREE

Tree

◆ One 4⅞" square, then cut an isosceles triangle (A).

◆ One 1½" x 2½" rectangle (C).

Background

◆ One 2¾" by at least 10½" strip. Fold and press end to end. Trim the rectangles 2¾" x 5¼", then cut in half diagonally (B). This will give you a set for another tree.

◆ Two 2" x 2½" rectangles (D).

See page 36 for more detailed instructions.

BASKET

Flowers

◆ Four 1¾" x 4¼" rectangles, then trim to 1¾" x 1¾" diamonds (A).

Basket

◆ One 3⅜" square, then cut in half diagonally (half-square triangles) (B). Use the extra for another basket.

◆ One 2⅝" square, then cut in half diagonally (half-square triangles) (C).

Background

◆ One 4⅜" square, then cut in half diagonally (half-square triangles) (D). Use the extra for another background.

◆ One 2¼" square (E).

◆ Two 2¼" x 3" rectangles (F).

◆ One 3¾" square, then cut in half diagonally twice (quarter-square triangles) (G). Use the extra two for another block background.

See page 38-39 for more detailed instructions.

WHIRLIGIG

◆ One 2⅛" x 28" strip (A).

◆ One 2⅛" x 28" strip (B).

◆ Four 3¾" equilateral triangles (C). Trim the block to measure 6½" x 7½".

See page 42-43 for more detailed instructions.

QUILT TOP CONSTRUCTION

1. Arrange your blocks following the photo on page 45.

2. Sew each row. Press. Sew all the rows together. Press.

Your quilt top should measure 24½" x 32½". If it does, use the instructions below to cut and attach the inner and outer border strips. If it doesn't, see page 22 to measure and cut the correct border lengths for your quilt top.

Inner and Outer Borders

1. Cut two 2½" x 32½" inner border strips and two 5½" x 32½" outer border strips.

2. Sew one inner border strip to one outer border strip along one long edge. Repeat for the other two strips. Press toward the inner border.

3. Sew one onto each side. Press toward the outer border.

4. Cut two 2½" x 24½" inner border strips and two 4½" x 24½" outer border strips.

5. Sew one inner border strip to one outer border strip along one long edge. Repeat for the other two strips. Press toward the inner border.

6. Sew a Whirligig block to each end of the top and bottom border strips matching the 6½" side of the block to the border. Press.

7. Sew onto the top and bottom. Press toward the inner border.

8. Layer, baste, and quilt as desired.

Quilt construction

47

Other Fine Books from C&T Publishing

Other books by Alex Anderson

Simply Stars
Start Quilting
Hand Quilting
Fabric Shopping
Hand Appliqué
Kids Start Quilting
Paper Piecing
Beautifully Quilted

15 Two-Block Quilts: Unlock the Secrets of Secondary Patterns, Claudia Olson

All About Quilting from A to Z, From the Editors and Contributors of Quilter's Newsletter Magazine and Quiltmaker Magazine

Along the Garden Path: More Quilters and Their Gardens, Jean & Valori Wells

America from the Heart: Quilters Remember September 11, 2001, Karey Bresenhan

App;iqué 12 Easy Ways!: Charming Quilts, Giftable Projects, & Timeless Techniques, Elly Sienkiewicz

At Home with Patrick Lose: Colorful Quilted Projects, Patrick Lose

Block Magic: Over 50 Fun & Easy Blocks from Squares and Rectangles, Nancy Johnson-Srebro

Block Magic, Too!: Over 50 NEW Blocks from Squares and Rectangles, Nancy Johnson-Srebro

Bouquet of Quilts, A: Garden-Inspired Projects for the Home, Edited by Jennifer Rounds & Cyndy Lyle Rymer

Color from the Heart: Seven Great Ways to Make Quilts with Colors You Love, Gai Perry

Contemporary Classics in Plaids & Stripes: 9 Projects from Piece 'O Cake Designs, Linda Jenkins & Becky Goldsmith

Cotton Candy Quilts: Using Feed Sacks, Vintage, and Reproduction Fabrics, Mary Mashuta

Cozy Cabin Quilts from Thimbleberries: 20 Projects for Any Home, Lynette Jensen

Create Your Own Quilt Labels!, Kim Churbuck

Easy Pieces: Creative Color Play with Two Simple Quilt Blocks, Margaret Miller

Elm Creek Quilts: Quilt Projects Inspired by the Elm Creek Quilts Novels, Jennifer Chiaverini & Nancy Odom

Fabric Stamping Handbook, The: •Fun Projects •Tips & Tricks •Unlimited Possibilities, Jean Ray Laury

Fantastic Fabric Folding: Innovative Quilting Projects, Rebecca Wat

Four Seasons in Flannel: 23 Projects— Quilts & More, Jean Wells & Lawry Thorn

From Fiber to Fabric: The Essential Guide to Quiltmaking Textiles, Harriet Hargrave

Hidden Block Quilts: • Discover New Blocks Inside Traditional Favorites • 13 Quilt Settings • Instructions for 76 Blocks, Lerlene Nevaril

In the Nursery: Creative Quilts and Designer Touches, Jennifer Sampou & Carolyn Schmitz

Magical Four-Patch and Nine-Patch Quilts, Yvonne Porcella

Mary Mashuta's Confetti Quilts: A No-Fuss Approach to Color, Fabric & Design, Mary Mashuta

New Sampler Quilt, The, Diana Leone

Photo Transfer Handbook, The: Snap It, Print It, Stitch It!, Jean Ray Laury

Q is for Quilt, Diana McClun & Laura Nownes

Quilts, Quilts, and More Quilts!, Diana McClun & Laura Nownes

Say It with Quilts, Diana McClun & Laura Nownes

Scrap Quilts: The Art of Making Do, Roberta Horton

Shadow Quilts, Patricia Magaret & Donna Slusser

Shoreline Quilts: 15 Glorious Get-Away Projects, compiled by Cyndy Rymer

Simple Fabric Folding for Christmas: 14 Festive Quilts & Projects, Liz Aneloski

Smashing Sets: Exciting Ways to Arrange Quilt Blocks, Margaret J. Miller

Stitch 'n Flip Quilts : 14 Fantastic Projects, Valori Wells

Stripes In Quilts, Mary Mashuta

Tradition with a Twist: Variations on Your Favorite Quilts, Blanche Young & Dalene Young-Stone

Travels with Peaky and Spike: Doreen Speckmann's Quilting Adventures, Doreen Speckmann

Wine Country Quilts: A Bounty of Flavorful Projects for Any Palette, Cyndy Lyle Rymer & Jennifer Rounds

For more information, write for a free catalog:
C&T Publishing, Inc.
P.O. Box 1456
Lafayette, CA 94549
(800) 284-1114
Email: ctinfo@ctpub.com
Website: www.ctpub.com

For quilting supplies:
Cotton Patch Mail Order
3405 Hall Lane, Dept.CTB
Lafayette, CA 94549
(800) 835-4418
(925) 283-7883
Email:quiltusa@yahoo.com
Website: www.quiltusa.com

Note: Fabrics used in the quilts shown may not be currently available since fabric manufacturers keep most fabrics in print for only a short time.